Volume 2

BRITISH RAILWAYS IN COLOUR

Alan Earnshaw & Kevin Derrick

Wester

6692

30

Nostalgia Road Publications

The **British Railways In Colour** Series ™

is produced under licence by

Nostalgia Road Publications Ltd.

Unit 6, Chancel Place

Shap Road Industrial Estate, Kendal LA9 6NZ

Tel. 01539 738832 - Fax: 01539 730075

designed and published by
Trans-Pennine Publishing Ltd.
PO Box 10,
Appleby-in-Westmorland,
Cumbria, CA16 6FA
Tel. 017683 51053 Fax. 017683 53558
e-mail: admin@transpenninepublishing.co.uk

and printed by
Kent Valley Colour Printers Ltd.
Kendal, Cumbria
01539 741344

© Trans-Pennine Publishing Ltd. 2004
Photographs: As credited

Front Cover: Epitomising the GWR's substantial mixed traffic fleet, 4914 *Cranmore Hall* is seen on the Devonian at Truro in 1962.
Trans-Pennine Archive (W196)

Rear Cover Top: Here we have 7029 *Clun Castle* at Old Oak Common in 1964 - a shed well frequented by enthusiasts and photographers of that time. Fortunately 7029 would go on into private preservation directly after her BR steam days had ended.
Bob Treacher, Alton Model Centre (W173)

Rear Cover Bottom: An 0-4-2 14xx class 1421 sits at Hemyock, in May 1963 with three six-wheel Express Dairy glass-lined milk tanks and a gas-lit ex-Barry Rly brake third coach four months before the passenger service ended. *Trans-Pennine Archive* (W301)

Title Page: Here we see a 56xx class, 6692, at Pensnett, Staffordshire in July 1963. This community west of Dudley was served by a small halt on the line that ran south from Oxley Junction, but full facilities were available at nearby Brierley Hill or Harts Hill on the line from Dudley (GW) to Stourbridge Junction.
Edward Dorricott (W224)

This Page: At Taunton in 1958 4-6-0 6004 *King George III* is on the Royal Duchy. *Trans-Pennine Archive* (W273)

WELCOME to the second volume of the **British Railways in Colour** series, which deals with what is most arguably the most well-liked of the British Railways regions. Whereas the London Midland was the largest of the regions, the Western always had an air of independence and a firm heritage that could be traced back to the original Great Western Railway - the largest of the pre-Grouped railways. Although that spirit of independence did not sit easily with other regions, nor the British Railway Board come to that, the Western Region did have some considerable reason for its very entrenched feelings of self-belief.

Above: *Here we see 7803* Barcote Manor *in near pristine condition, at Shrewsbury's No.4 platform waiting with an Aberystwyth train in 1963.* Trans-Pennine Archive (W259)

Exponents of the GWR or Western Region may well point to its proud steam locomotives or even its temperamental diesel-hydraulics as the source of their pride, but serious students of railway history will know that the GWR was simply the safest railway in the world; as its pioneering use of Automatic Train Control set safety standards that the other railways could only envy!

3

Above: King Class 6004 *King George III* is seen again, this time at Chipping Sodbury on 16th December 1961 with the Red Dragon. The 'new town' of Chipping Sodbury can be traced back to the mid 12th century when a William Crassus, then owner of the Sodbury estates decided to encourage an urban development. He chose a site on a small hill above the River Frome and its two mills, where two important trading routes crossed. Conversely, railways came very late to the town, and also finished early with the loss of the passenger station in 1961.
Gordon Brown (W331)

Right: For years the nearest railway station had been at Yate on the Midland Railway, but with the creation of the London to South Wales railway Sodbury began to witness the railway era from 1897 onwards. The main work around the town was the construction of the Sodbury Tunnel, but the station did not open until July 1903. As a through express route, named trains were a regular sight at Chipping Sodbury, and a few minutes later, after capturing *King George III*, the photographer recorded the passage of 4081 *Warwick Castle* on the Capitals United.
Gordon Brown (W261)

Top Left: Although the Western Region carried the named trains theme with great panache, not all its express services were bestowed with such adornments. Here we visit Bath Spa, to see a pair of named locomotives on un-named services. First of all we see 6918 *Sandon Hall* on the 4.35pm Salisbury - Bristol, in May 1963. This service connected at Bath, with the service to Calne (Wiltshire), which by this date had already been dieselised. The DMU for this branch, seen to the left of the Hall class 4-6-0 would probably stop en-route at the delightfully-named Black Dog Halt. The Calne branch lost its goods services during 1964, and was severed completely from the railway network on 20th September 1965.
Alan Pike OBE (W204)

Bottom Left: Staying in Bath on the same day, the photographer found 5043 *Earl of Mount Edgecumbe* powering out of the station. This was the first of the Castle Class 4-6-0 to be named after an Earl. Bath was, of course, a major railway town in its heyday, with the Great Western, Midland and Somerset & Dorset Joint Railway all providing services, but the London & South Western Railway's plans to reach Bath came to nothing. In the days of railway mania, south and west Wiltshire were important areas of sheep farming and woollen manufacturing, and these two staple industries provided much potential traffic for the embryonic carriers. Towards the end of the 19th Century this trade began to decline quite rapidly, and the railways became rural backwaters, and thus ripe for closure under Beeching.
Alan Pike OBE (W266)

Top Right: The GWR's policy of naming locomotives, continued by the Western Region was again another popular move with both enthusiasts and the travelling public alike. However by 1964, the British Railways Board was very definitely seeing the influence of its new Chairman Dr. Richard Beeching, as both named trains and locomotive nameplates began to disappear. A good example of this is seen with 6859 *Yiewsley Grange*, which has been stripped of its nameplates. It is pictured passing the splendid gas-holders at Banbury. Quite a few of the Grange class locomotives were transferred into the Midland Region along with their home sheds at places like Oxley and Tyseley. As a whole the class lasted well, and the first of these to be cut up was 6801 *Aylburton Grange*, which died at Swindon Works at the end of 1960.
Bob Treacher, Alton Model Centre (W203)

Bottom Right: More symbols of Victorian technology are seen in this undated view as the gas-holders provide the back-drop to 57xx 0-6-0PT 3769 at Shrewsbury. Introduced from 1929 onwards, this versatile pannier tank was a development of the 2021 class. This particular member had been at Wolverhampton Stafford Road for a couple of years in the late 1950s, moving to Chester Great Western Shed for a brief spell in 1958 before moving down the Welsh Marches in January 1959. It remained at Shrewsbury for a couple of years before becoming an Oswestry engine during 1961-2. It was finally withdrawn in October 1962 and was sent to Swindon where it stayed for a short while before being cut up in December 1963.
Trans-Pennine Archive (W119)

Above: Continuing our thoughts of locomotives associated with former Cambrian Railway sheds, we now see 6378 a 63xx class Mogul 2-6-0 at Welshpool in the early 1960s. For several years this engine was based at Machynlleth, a town that was deeply affected when several of its prominent citizens were killed in the Abermule railway disaster which occurred when two trains met head-on whilst travelling at speed on a single track line on 26th January 1921.
Trans-Pennine Archive (W278)

Right: The crash claimed 17 lives, as a consequence of an error caused by some very slack working of the Tyer signalling system at Abermule Station. Not in the least surprising, the official report into the disaster was extremely critical of both the company and its staff. The crash on the near bankrupt railway took place at the exact point where Manor class 4-6-0, 7819 *Hinton Manor*, passes with the Cambrian Coast Express on 19th September 1963.
Richard Icke (W233)

Left: The stunning scenery found in mid-Wales was also rivalled by other locations on the GWR, and down in the West Country counties like Devon offered passengers many fine vistas from the carriage window. Always of interest on any journey through Devon was the hive of activity around the station and engine shed at Newton Abbott, as pictured here in June 1959. Here we see a work-stained 6921 *Borwick Hall* along with a Royal Mail Travelling Post Office coach that we can just observe behind it. Note the fact that the locomotive has just a single headlamp on the buffer beam!
Alan Pike OBE (W219)

Above: Again at Newton Abbott on the same date, 6th June 1959, we see a very busy scene. This of course had not been just a station and locomotive depot, but had also been a locomotive works as well, and it was judged a strategic target by the German Luftwaffe, who bombed it during World War II. The two 51xx 2-6-2 tank engines seen here, 5183 (pictured left with the Kingswear local) and 5154 (right), would both end their days far away from the tranquillity of rural Devon. They were in fact cut up in the scrapyard of Cashmores, Great Bridge Street, Birmingham along with a great many other GWR locomotives.
Alan Pike OBE (W286)

Above: Although unlike the beauty of rural Devon, the industrialised heart of the Midlands was nevertheless an important centre for photographers in the 1960s. Not too far from where those West Country 51xx Prairie tank engines would eventually be dismantled, we see King Class 6020 *King Henry IV* approaching platforms 7 and 8 of Snow Hill Station with a Wolverhampton to Paddington train. *Richard Icke* (W186)

Right: Also in the West Midlands, this time taking the relief road from Birmingham Moor Street, we see a modified Hall class 4-6-0, 7908 *Henshall Hall* as it passes Bordesley on a Summer Saturday extra. This engine was built by BR in January 1950 and was first allocated to Bristol, St. Philip's Marsh. Its last shed allocation was Tyseley, from where it was withdrawn in October 1965, before being scrapped at Cashmore's, Great Bridge. *Richard Icke* (W153)

Top Left: Doctor Foster went to Gloucester, or so goes the children's rhyme, but in railway terms it seemed every one wanted to get there. Like Birmingham, the city was seen as an important staging post for the railway companies. This left it with a legacy of having parentage of both the GWR and LMS. However, it firmly became part of the Western Region after nationalisation. This trio of pictures reflects this management, starting just north of the city with an 87xx pannier tank at Churchdown in 1964. These reliable 0-6-0PTs typified local branch and shunting locomotive across the Western Region, and thus eptomise the very essence of the GWR.
Chris Forrest (W121)

Bottom Left: Gloucester had two principal stations, Central (GWR) and Midland (MR/LMS). This view shows Central Station on 26th September 1963 with 63xx Mogul 6368 on a passenger train from Hereford and 6877 *Llanfair Grange* on a freight. Note the scissors cross-over in the foreground, along with the small telephone box that allowed contact with the signal box.
Richard Icke (W156)

Right: Waiting to depart from Gloucester Central with a Hereford stopping train on 15th September 1964, we see 41xx Prairie tank engine, 4107. The route it would take north east in Herefordshire was one of the prettiest railway lines in the country, meandering through the stunning scenery. After crossing the county boundary near Mitcheldean Road, it would then pass on through the incredibly beautiful Ross-on-Wye.
Chris Forrest (W137)

Top Left: The strong rivalry of the relationship between the GWR and the LMS in areas like Gloucester can be easily understood as the railways vied with one another for traffic. The Grouping of the railways in 1923 had already eliminated much of the rivalry that existed between the various small companies and concentrated them into the four larger groups. The nationalisation of 1948 was 'supposed' to eliminate these forever, but this was not always the case in practice. In locomotive facilities the railways tended to be centralised, with all the sheds in a given district going under one or another of the new regions. A good example of this was the former GWR shed at Banbury (84C), which from 1963 found itself under Midland Region control (2D). Here a former GWR 72xx class 2-8-2T, 7207, is seen at the shed in 1964. It was withdrawn in November of that year and actually cut up on site by Friswell's of Banbury, as it was classed as being unfit to be moved by rail to their yard. *Win Wall - Strathwood Library Collection* (W115)

Bottom Left: Another shed transferred from the Western Region to the Midland Region was Croes Newydd, which changed from 84J (89B from 1961) to 6C in 1963. The Midland Region closed the shed in 1967, two years after this picture of 57xx 0-6-0PT 4683 was taken on 17th January 1965. It is seen amongst other former Western locomotives, proudly wearing its 6C shed code plate. However, the once-immaculate surroundings at the shed seem to be long-forgotten as they are (by then) especially unkempt as steam draws towards its last days.
Chris Forrest (W177)

Top Right: Returning once again to Devon we see a 14xx class 0-4-2T, 1471, on a one-coach Autocar train on the Hemyock Branch in the Spring of 1963. The Autocar train was a classic GWR development of the 'push and pull' concept that was applied by many railways in the days before diesel multiple units. The ability for the driver to work the train either from the footplate or from a cab at the end of the Autocar carriage was a very practical approach to the operation of branch lines or lightly patronised rural railways. In many ways the idea was copied from the British tramway operators, where a driving position was provided at either end of the tramcar. Connection between the driving position of the Autocar coach and the footplate of the locomotive was by means of a series of rods that ran below the coach.
Trans-Pennine Archive (W129)

Bottom Right: By way of contrast to the humble 14xx-Autocar, we now see another aspect of the GWR services down in the West Country as Castle Class 5023 *Brecon Castle* arrives at Totnes with a six-coach train in June 1959. Just look at the 'wealth' of railway infrastructure that surrounds 5023 as the train draws into the platform. The large timber-built warehouse in the background saw a large quantity of agricultural traffic over the years; for instance, this view shows a newly delivered and pristine-looking muck spreader standing on the dock alongside. The shed is also worthy of note, because it is a mute reminder that this section of the South Devon Railway was once served by broad gauge trains.
Alan Pike OBE (W182)

Left: On 12th June 1963 we have yet another Castle, this time a double-chimney member of the class. This one, 7018 *Drysllyn Castle*, was one of the BR-built examples of the class. It is pictured outside the substantial coaling and water stage at London's Old Oak Common MPD where it was based. This facility obviously reflected the importance of the Western line into Paddington, and it was designed to quickly deal with engines coming off and going on to trains at the terminal station.
Strathwood Library Collection (W189)

Top Right: By way of contrast, the stage at Leamington was rather more basic, as can be seen in this picture dating from 2nd December 1962. It shows a 56xx 0-6-2T, 5658, which was a member of a class that was predominantly associated with South Wales, but was also seen in smaller numbers at other locations as well.
Rickard Icke (W127)

Bottom Right: The use of the 56xx class locomotives in Wales was due to their undoubted ability at handling heavily laden coal trains up fairly severe gradients. The Welsh valley lines proved to be ideal territory for them, and 6622 is seen on the former Rhymney Railway line. Stored at Rhymney shed in 1964, the class was quickly decimated despite being intact up until the end of 1962 as diesel locomotives and diminishing traffic affected their traditional duties. Many were stored at Rhymney until the South Wales scrapyards like Birds, Cashmores and Hayes could make serious in-roads into their numbers.
Win Wall - Strathwood Library Collection Collection (W210)

Above: Staying with the theme of engines from South Wales, we move on to one of those small batches of engines that were transferred to work in the South West in the summer of 1961 when there were insufficient new diesels available to work the summer schedule. Here we have 7224, a 72xx 2-8-2T that was sent from Aberdare to Exeter in June 1961, before being sent back to Ebbw Junction in November 1961. A year later it was the first of its class to be withdrawn (along with 7241), and after a period of storage it was despatched to the scrapyards, being cut by Hayes at Bridgend. As this yard was so close to places where the 72xx engines worked, this was quite understandable.
Alan Pike OBE (W164)

Right: A type of Great Western tank that was more commonly associated with the West Country, but seen here in the Principality of Wales is the 45xx class 2-6-2T. These tank engines were for many years associated with the B-set coaches, but as diesel multiple units became available, they were finally displaced from their traditional duties and were either dispersed to other areas or withdrawn for scrap. This view shows that 4557 has escaped on to the long rural branch that ran 27.5 miles from Whitland to Cardigan, which has yet to be fully dieselised. Seen with the estuary in the background, the engine could be mistaken for thinking it was back home in Cornwall.
Richard Icke (W118)

Left: Talking of transferred engines, we might think that this picture shows the ultimate in transfers, as what we have here is actually a Midland Region station, on what was once a Great Central line, and has a Great Western locomotive in the view. Like the previous picture, we again see an ex-GWR tank engine (this time 1432) taking water near the signal box. It is seen here in 1961, at Wrexham Central. The GWR station was known as Wrexham General, but there was also a Cambrian/GCR joint station called Exchange. That station also transferred to the London Midland Region, but it was closed in 1982. *Strathwood Library Collection* (W116)

Above: The themes of watering facilities and the 14xx class continue in this picture of 1421 taking on supplies at Hemyock in Devon. The view dates from May 1963, some four months before passenger services were discontinued, however the line remained open for freight traffic until November 1975. The staple traffic on this line was always associated with milk and produce trains, which were run from the Express Dairies Creamery at Hemyock. From there milk would be despatched to London in the type of milk tankers seen in this 'mixed' train, and it was one of the few places in the country where such trains would be run. *Trans-Pennine Archive* (W199)

Above: Milk tankers and 'Siphons' would often be coupled on to West Country express services, and in effect these express-rated 'freight' vehicles would be seen on passenger trains. Not all of the expresses had 'mixed' traffic, but this one certainly has a mixture of carriage liveries, ranging from carmine and cream, to chocolate and cream and BR maroon, as County Class 4-6-0 1002 *County of Berks* waits at St. Erth in September 1959. Note the signals to the left of the picture
the late Norman Browne, Strathwood Library Collection (W124)

Right: St. Erth was also the junction for the St. Ives branch, and looking from the footbridge (seen in the background of the above picture), this view shows the station in the opposite direction. Approaching the station is modified Hall 7921 *Eddstone Hall*, which is bound for Penzance in September 1959. Note the parcels traffic, stored on the station handcart, which has probably come off the branch train and looks to be destined for the nearby town of Penzance.
the late Norman Browne, Strathwood Library Collection (W305)

Left: Another famous West Country junction was that found at Brent, where the attractive branch to Kingsbridge diverged from the main line. Here we see Hall class 4920 *Dumbleton Hall* which, in June 1959, was a Newton Abbott-based locomotive. Although it travelled around quite a lot in its last few years of existence as a BR engine, it was essentially a Devonian resident and in preservation it would prove this by returning to the county and the Dart Valley Railway after being sold to Woodham Brothers scrapyard in February 1966.
Alan Pike OBE (W184)

Above: Staying at Brent again in June 1959 we see 6873 *Caradoc Grange* arriving with another train of very mixed-livery stock. It may not look like it from this delightfully sunny picture, but Brent has an unusual place in the history of the GWR, for it was here that passengers were stranded for several days during the Great Blizzard of 1891. An express heading through Brent was derailed by an exceptionally heavy snowdrift, and was stuck for several days until the track could be cleared. Ironically this event was not even in the dead of winter, but the month of March. *Alan Pike OBE* (W225)

Top Left: Under British Railways' ownership, many reminders of the old GWR were to be seen, but a full 14 years into nationalised ownership, and 9709 still retains its original GWR lettering on the tank sides. It was one of a sub-class of 11 57xx class 0-6-0PTs fitted with condensing equipment for working on the Metropolitan widened lines under west London. Apart from 9707, which went to Taunton in 1964, they very rarely travelled beyond the capital and were all based at Old Oak Common. Overhauls were either at Swindon or Wolverhampton, and they were rare catches for the spotters who caught them on their travels. One of those that went to Wolverhampton 9708 in 1958 was not returned as it was condemned and scrapped at the works in 1959. The last of the sub-class, 9706, lasted until 1964, but 9709 was withdrawn in 1962 and sold to Cashmore's of Newport.
Trans-Pennine Archive (W175)

Bottom Left: The spirit of 'Western Pride' was evident right down to the end of steam in the region, even though officialdom did much to discourage this. On 9th October 1965 we see Grange 6861 *Crynant Grange* devoid of all its plates at Banbury (by then a Midland Region shed). Remarkably the engine still retains the elite atmosphere of the GWR, and compared to many of its contemporaries of that time it looks remarkably clean and the copper fittings are still in situ. It was built in February 1939 and first allocated to Bristol. It was last allocated to Tyseley and withdrawn October 1965 before being scrapped at Cohens of Kettering.
Michael Beeton (W138)

Above: Another immaculate-looking engine is seen here with 4-6-0, 7011, which (with a name like *Banbury Castle*) suggests it should perhaps have been kept at the previously discussed shed and not Worcester. This is one of the BR-built Castles and it is paired with a Hawksworth tender. It was out-shopped in June 1948, but had a relatively short working life as it was withdrawn in February 1965. It was first allocated to Bristol Bath Road shed when new, and it spent a long number of years there (until the early 1960s at least). It then went to Worcester where it is pictured before finally ending up at Oxley Shed. It was sent there for the last summer of steam traction on the Western Region of BR and this saw it working some of the Summer holiday 'extras' from the Midlands to the West Country, which had previously been the preserve of Oxley MPD's Stanier Class 5 4-6-0s. For 1964 the shed received a trio of Britannia Class 4-6-0s at the start of the summer timetable, 70045 *Lord Rowallan*, the unnamed 70047 and 70053 *Moray Firth*, followed by the two transfers from Worcester 7011 *Banbury Castle* and 7023 *Penrice Castle* in June. Enthusiasts thus got a chance to say farewell to the rapidly dwindling Castle class as the survivors saw intensive action between June and September that year.
Win Wall, Strathwood Library Collection (W220)

Above: In the next pair of views we look at the steeply graded banks at Hatton and Gresford. The gradient at the first of these locations varied between 1:95 and 1:110, and involved a four-mile climb from Warwick to Hatton Junction, although there were a couple of relatively level sections to make life a little easier for the locomotive crews. Here the engine is King Class 4-6-0, 6026 *King John* in June 1960.
Strathwood Library Collection (W12)

Right: Moving on to Gresford, which was much further along the Paddington - Birmingham - Chester -Birkenhead route, another climb was encountered 184 miles from London. This was a 1:82.5 gradient that descended for around 3.5 miles towards Chester from Wrexham, and where we see Hall class 6934 *Beacham Well Hall* on 31st July 1964 on a fitted goods service. This would be around a year before the engine was withdrawn in October 1965 and sold to Cashmores for scrap. *Chris Forrest* (W3)

Left: The larger Prairie tank engines were widely distributed until their progressive withdrawal from 1958 onwards, when Swindon began cutting up these 2-6-2Ts. Many of the class had gone by 1962, but 6128 was a survivor until March of 1965, when it was withdrawn at Gloucester (85B) and subsequently despatched by Birds of Bridgend that August. This engine, seen here with the cat on the wheel badge and a very clean un-lined black livery, would surely have been one of the last to wear a livery of this kind on the BR system?
Trans-Pennine Archive (W197)

Above: One of the last sheds to employ the large Prairies was Oxford, and another clean engine is seen at the city's station in August 1959. Here we see 5961 *Toynbee Hall* with a rake of Southern Region green stock on an unidentified inter-regional working. At this time this particular Hall was based at Llanelly (87F), and at first it seems a rather unusual combination of motive power and stock. It would, in most probability, be a Birkenhead to Folkstone or Margate working which employed SR and WR stock on alternate days.
the late Norman Browne, Strathwood Library Collection (W178)

Above: Here we see Manor Class 4-6-0 7809 *Childrey Manor* at Ellesmere on the former Cambrian line south of Wrexham Central. At the time of this 1960 picture, the Grange was a Wrexham (GW) engine, and the shed plate 84K can just be made out from the grime on the smoke-box door. Ellesmere was quite an important junction station, as it was here where the Wrexham line diverged from the Cambrian route between Whitchurch and Oswestry. Note the porter as he bustles along the platform in the days before un-staffed halts. *Trans-Pennine Archive* (W212)

Right: Once again the porter is prominent in this view at Bala Town, as 57xx 0-6-0PT 9669 arrives with stopping train for Bala Junction on 14th November 1961. The role of the porter in steam days could alternate from periods of frantic activity, to long-spells of doing nothing. Fortunately, most station workers also took great pride in their charges, and the porters, booking clerks and the like would often spend many hours working on the station's gardens and general appearance; again a contrast to the un-staffed halts of today! *Richard Icke* (W269)

Top Left: The steep banks found on the Western Region, especially in the south west were a source of continual working difficulty! So, in the late 1930s when Merz & MacLellan were asked to write a feasibility study for electrifying the main line with the sole purpose of avoiding the need for banking engines. In many instances the GWR used pilot engines on its more difficult climbs, but the gradient at Lickey (inherited from the Midland Region in 1958) had traditionally used engines pushing from the rear. The most famous of these being 58100, the huge Midland 0-10-0 better known as 'Big Bertha'. In BR days a variety of other types were allocated to Bromsgrove MPD for this duty including LMS Jintys, 96xx pannier tanks and BR 9F 2-10-0s. Here we see 4981 *Abberley Hall* undertaking the bank as a train engine, with 0-6-0PT, 8409, working hard behind.
John Gill (W336)

Bottom Left: The 94xx had a power classification of 4F, whereas the ex-LMS 0-6-0T Jintys that had been used by the Midland Region were just to the 3F classification. Both the Jintys and the pannier tanks were often used in tandem behind the heaviest trains, but in this case *Abberley Hall* needs only the assistance of one locomotive. In terms of power the Jinty was classed as being equal to one locomotive, whereas the 94xx class was counted as being equal to one and a half locomotives, whilst the 52xx class were equal to two locomotives and the 9Fs three. This was the system used by the Bromsgrove signalman to decide how many banking engines were needed for any given train.
John Gill (W291)

Top Right: To illustrate the power of the BR Standard Class 9F 2-10-0s at Lickey, we now turn to Campden Bank on the Oxford to Worcester line. Situated between Moreton-in-the-Marsh and Honeybourne, this bank climbed for around four miles at 1:100 and had a long tunnel near its summit just for fun. In contrast to the summer time shots at Lickey, the views at Campden are decidedly autumnal as 92226 powers up the hill with a rake of 16-ton mineral wagons behind it. Whereas 9Fs were used at Bromsgrove for banking duties at Lickey, here one of the class takes the role of train engine whilst banking is provided by 0-6-0 2244 from the 22xx class. The date of this view, and that of the second is 2nd November 1964.
John Newman (B178)

Bottom Right: Taken a few minutes later, this view shows the tail end of the train. In previous times the banker would have probably been buffered up to a traditional GWR 20-ton 'Toad' brake-van, but by the early 1960s these, like the branch lines, were then very much in decline. The brake-van seen here next to the 22xx banker is one built to an LMS pattern. Provided with a veranda at both ends, these tended to be more practical than the GWR models. However, on a day such as this, we can be sure that the guard would have probably preferred to stay inside, and thus make full use of the duckets provided on either side of his van. The little cast-iron stove inside the guard's domain would have provided a warmer environment, but the van would nevertheless still be quite draughty and not especially comfortable.
John Newman (W297)

Left: The winter weather has certainly set in on our next view of a traditional GWR freight engine. To illustrate this we see a 28xx class 2-8-0, which was the improved version by Collett (and referred to by some as the 2884 class). It had the improved cab with side windows and slightly better working conditions for the crew, which would certainly be most welcome on days like this. The Hereford-bound freight is approaching Severn Bridge Junction, with its stately signal box on 2nd December 1962.
Richard Icke (W151)

Above: On a much more pleasant day, the photographer takes a picture of County Class 4-6-0 1026, *County of Salop* at Shrewsbury as she waits to head for the Cambrian Coast in 1962. The scene he captured is typical of the day, but not long afterwards the over-all roof would be swept away and even the 4-6-0 would be withdrawn from its home shed of Shrewsbury. Sadly this class of GWR 4-6-0 saw no examples being sent to Woodhams of Barry, and so none of them escaped into preservation.
Trans-Pennine Archive (W146)

Above: As the County class was enjoying holiday traffic in its last summer, here we see a Modified Hall 6971 *Athelhampton Hall* at Barry Island on 15th July 1962. The scene is so typical of the transitional years, as a DMU waits alongside, whilst buses line up outside the station. This working is an excursion from the West Midlands to Barry Island, but the ensuing years would see many visitors heading to the station to see the large numbers of redundant steam locomotives that were stockpiled on the old sidings around Barry Docks, whilst waiting their turn to enter the local scrapyards. One of these was the yard of Woodham Brothers, which has a significant place in railway history thanks to the number of engines that were **not** scrapped. *Richard Icke* (W327)

Right: As Barry Island is a well-known name in railway history, so too was Pontypool Road due to its role as a major junction, albeit in the middle of nowhere. In fact, because this station sprang up miles from any major community, it took its name from the Pontypool road that passed by the site. A shed was opened at the junction that became established here, and it remained operational as a steam shed until the spring of 1965, although it had gone completely by the October of 1967. Seen resting at the shed in August 1964 is 3708, a 57xx class 0-6-0PT, which had been a long-term resident of the shed. It went to store at Ebbw Junction in May 1965, later to be scrapped by Cashmores of Newport.
Win Wall, Strathwood Library Collection (W401)

Above: Contrasting with the rural shed at Pontypool Road, we move to Southall, West London. This shed (81C) was thoroughly modernised in 1955, with the coming of diesel traction in mind, but it stayed as a steam depot until September 1965. In theory it closed completely in November 1968 when its allocation was removed, but nevertheless it remained a stabling point for the London Divison DMU fleet.

After this the DMU fleet cascaded to Reading, and up to the time of writing the depot remains a preservation centre although there have been concerted moves to re-develop this piece of prime real-estate. Here we see 4700 doyen of the 47xx class 2-8-0s and Hall class 4976 *Warfield Hall*, resting on shed with their 81C plates in the summer of 1962, with an unidentified 57xx 0-6-0 PT alongside.
Trans-Pennine Archive (W215)

Below: Southall was always a good place for 'foreign' visitors, notably London Midland Region engines in BR steam days. Here we see a Hughes/Fowler 2-6-0 'Crab' 42848, which for a long time was a Manchester Longsight engine. This picture thus provides a link for the two authors of this book as Alan Earnshaw was a regular visitor to Longsight, whereas Southall was home territory for Kevin Derrick.

The long distance freights from the north took many trains down to the West Yard at Southall, and the engines would then run down to 81C for servicing before their return home. In later years, Southall also became a resting point for London Midland Region engines destined for scrapping in South Wales. This view dates from February 1965, when the 6P 5F loco was based at Edge Hill (8A). *Strathwood Library Collection* (W417)

Left: Some engines spent their working lives moving from shed to shed, and these were quite often the bad steamers who a Shed Master was quite happy to pass on to an unsuspecting colleague, whereas good engines often stayed for years at the same shed. One such example is 43xx 2-6-0 Mogul, 6343, which was a long time Taunton (83B) engine. It is found here at its local station, where the single line tablet equipment can be seen on the side of the tender. This engine was a regular on the Barnstaple line, although it was used on the West Somerset (at least in the summer of 1958). The picture dates from the summer of 1959 and 6343 was to be withdrawn just over a year later in September 1960. *Trans-Pennine Archive* (W150)

Above: Another 43xx, but this time an unidentified member of the class, as it travels at speed with a mixed freight train that includes China Clay hoods on the main line near Plymouth in June 1959. Just discernable in the picture is the site of Laira Halt (closed in 1930), where the remains of the stairway leading down to the under-pass (and thus to Laira engine sheds) can be clearly seen. The engine sheds themselves would become one of the status symbols of the modernised railway in the 1960s, as they would undergo complete rebuilding to provide facilities for the diesel locomotives that were being progressively introduced on the Western Region.
Alan Pike OBE (W195)

45

Above: Whereas the new Laira shed was a bright and airy locomotive depot in the 1960s, the Western Region's 'premier' shed at Old Oak Common (81A) was a much more ethereal affair. Here we visit the shed and see a really atmospheric scene in one of the three round-houses. From left to right, we see Grange Class 6863 *Dolhywell Grange*, Hall Class 6942 *Eshton Hall*, Castle Class 5057 *Earl Waldegrave* and Castle Class 7029, *Clun Castle*, surely the most photographed of Western Region engines.
Win Wall - Strathwood Library Collection (W187)

Right: A second view inside Old Oak Common in July 1963 with a cluster of engines round the turntable; from left to right an unidentified double-chimney Castle class 4-6-0, followed by County Class 1024 *County of Pembroke*, then pannier tank 3754, condenser-fitted pannier tank 9706 and 'Tanner One' 61xx class 2-6-2T, 6142. This scene was captured on what was obviously a lovely day outside as the sunlight filters through the grimy roof windows, giving a curious dappled light inside the shed.
Win Wall - Strathwood Library Collection (SH81)

Left: Worcester MPD (85A) was renowned for the first class way in which it turned out its locomotives, but this is not well illustrated in this picture of a rather work-stained Castle Class 4-6-0, 5054 *Earl of Ducie* on 7th June 1964. The engine carries the single chimney and has a Hawksworth tender paired with it at the time of this view, and it therefore makes an interesting comparison with its sister engine seen in the next picture.
Win Wall - Strathwood Library Collection (W172)

Above: Two years earlier, we see 5034, *Corfe Castle* at Old Oak Common with a double chimney and a Collett tender. The contrast between the two types of tender is well illustrated with this view as 5034 is buffered up to another engine with a Hawksworth tender. It has to be said, however, that the tenders were not permanently paired to a given locomotive, and they were often swapped over when going into the works for attention.
Trans-Pennine Archive (W130

Above: Displaying this picture large may not appeal to readers who are not interested in views of nameplates. Yet this view is very significant as it shows the way in which the Great Western decided to commemorate its passing into BR, as this was the last Castle to be built under their control. Generally the Castle 4-6-0s were named after a literal castle, abbey or an Earl, but a few were named after Battle of Britain aircraft. The names also incorporated famous GWR personalities, but oddly that of Collett was not included in the prestigious listing, we wonder why? The oddball was 7005, *Sir Edward Elgar,* although its name would be later perpetuated on a Class 50 for the GWR 150 celebrations (see our book on this subject). When 7037 was named *Swindon* and 7007 *Great Western,* the name of this great railway and its famous works were thus perpetuated into the nationalised railway era. Note that the coat of arms of the GWR appears below the nameplate.

the late Norman Browne, Strathwood Library Collection (W221)

Top Right: This time the view shows the entire locomotive (7007 *Great Western*) with a rake of chocolate and cream stock at Sonning in 1961. The cutting at Sonning was a popular location for photographers in the 1950s and '60s, but the majority used an overbridge further along from where this view was taken. Located some 34 miles from Paddington, and two miles from Reading, this was one of the locations you could guarantee to find named express trains racing along the four-track section. There was an additional block section on this part of the route, as the small cabin at Sonning could be switched in to provide additional capacity at times of peak traffic, notably summer Saturdays.
Trans-Pennine Archive (W200)

Bottom Right: On the same day, but looking in the opposite direction, we see a Hall class 4-6-0 on the fast line. With what seems an excess use of motive power for just three parcels vans, 5987 *Brocket Hall* makes light work of the duty. The lineside hut and the neatness of the formation on the permanent way show the pride that the local ganger has put into his work. What a shame that railways of today do not reflect the same high standards! The locomotive was also one of a group that had a reason to be proud, as it was a member of the London Division allocation, and during BR days most of its life was spent at sheds in the 81 group, these included Old Oak Common (81A), Reading (81D), Didcot (81E) and Oxford (81F). It was at the latter shed where it ended its days in January 1964 before being cut up at Swindon that August.
Trans-Pennine Archive (W241)

Above: The versatility of the Hall class 4-6-0s meant that they lasted well into the 1960s, and at the end of 1961 only ten had been scrapped or condemned. Yet in 1962 it began in earnest and 73 went that year, just 14 were left at the end of 1964 and by December 1965 they were all gone. In this 1961 view we see 5932 *Haydon Hall* which at the time was allocated to Old Oak Common (81A), it is seen there in this view (with a Castle class 4-6-0) behind outside the new office accommodation that was provided at the depot in the late 1950s. It was an Old Oak Common engine from at least 1957 to April 1963, when it was allocated to Reading. After that it travelled around a number of depots before being withdrawn from Barrow Road, Bristol 82E in August 1965. *Trans-Pennine Archive* (W208)

Right: The Modified Hall class 4-6-0s were fairly good survivors too, and with the exception of just six engines, the class remained intact until 1964. A large batch were based at Oxford, but these went at the end of 1965. In total just eight were cut up at Swindon and the bulk of them (20) were cut at Cashmore's scrapyard in Newport. The engine pictured, 6994, here at Thame was a member of the fifth batch of Modified Halls and was named *Baggrave Hall*. At the time of this 1960 view it was one of the 16 members of the class that were allocated to Oxford and it is from there that it has set out on a working for Risborough; this service was to last until 7th January 1963 when passenger trains were withdrawn. *Trans-Pennine Archive* (W300)

Above: For most of its later BR life this Churchward 28xx class 2-8-0 was at Severn Tunnel Junction (86E), although nationalisation had found it at Cardiff Canton when the GWR handed it over to the newly formed British Railways on 1st January 1948. Its duties would however have been vaguely familiar, and as seen here, it was the ponderously slow loose-coupled freight trains that it suited best. Pictured at Chippenham in April 1962 not long before it was withdrawn and placed in store at Severn Tunnel Junction. It languished there for three months but at the end of the summer it was decided that there was no further requirement for the engine and it was consigned to Swindon who commenced cutting in late August 1962. *Alan Pike OBE* (W190)

Below: In November 1958 our photographer visited Gloucester and captured a number of classic views of the station. Here we see 14xx class 0-4-2T with a pair of Autocar trailers. The liveries of the two cars are decidedly different, with the leading car being freshly painted and the trailing car being in the earlier BR red and bearing a name, which is probably *Thrush*.

This may well be a train for the Ledbury branch, on which 0-4-2Ts and Autocars were used to supplement the GWR AEC railcars that had been introduced in 1940. The route to Ledbury was 19 miles long and roughly followed the course of the Herefordshire and Gloucestershire Canal that opened in 1798 and was taken over by the GWR in 1876. *Trans-Pennine Archive* (W170)

Top Left: Our next port of call is Bath Green Park, the northern terminus of the Somerset & Dorset Joint Railway. This view, taken at Whitsuntide 1963 shows that the line had a very interesting period of ownership. The nominally independent Somerset & Dorset had a complex history in which both the London & South Western and Midland railways played a significant part. In the 1930s, the LMS assumed even greater responsibility for the line, but on nationalisation in 1948 it became part of the Southern Region, and this influence is confirmed by the rake of Bullied coaching stock behind Standard Class 3MT 2-6-2T 82004. Yet by the time this picture was taken, the S&D had become the responsibility of the Western Region, a fact that is evident from the station's enamelled nameboards in chocolate and cream and the locomotiove being painted in BR lined green after a Swindon repair. *Trans-Pennine Archive* (B221)

Bottom Left: As Swindon Works had a big part in the building of BR standard classes, it is not surprising that the standards were to be seen in all parts of the Western Region, where they displaced older GWR designs. However, not all the standards that were allocated to the Western Region originated from Swindon, as we see here with 4MT 2-6-4T, 80069 at Swansea Victoria in 1962. Although the station has become part of the Western Region, it was originally opened by the LNWR on the route that came down to South Wales through Pontardulais. Both the LNWR and the Midland made incursions into the heart of the GWR in search of the rich coal traffic that existed there. *Trans-Pennine Archive* (W216)

Top Right: We return to Taunton in 1958, when Kings and Castles were the regular performers to and from the West Country. Here our photographer captures a Castle Class 4-6-0 4089 *Donnington Castle*. This locomotive was built at Swindon in 1925, not long after the Grouping, and was first allocated to the top link at Old Oak Common. It had a working life of almost 40 years, finally being withdrawn from Reading (81D) in September 1964. By that time it had also been paired with a Hawksworth tender.
Trans-Pennine Archive (W73)

Bottom Right: Taunton will always be associated with the accident that befell 6028 *King George VI* on the night of 4th November 1940. Whilst working a Penzance train, it was put on to the slow lines as far as Norton Fitzwarren, but the crew did not realise this and continued at a speed of 40mph. As another train was being allowed to pass it on the fast line, the slow line points were set towards the buffers. The 4-6-0 crashed through these and rolled down a bank, killing 26 passengers. Originally named *King Henry II* its name had only been changed in 1937 to that of the new monarch after the abdication of King Edward VIII. As a matter of prestige the 4-6-0 was recovered from its boggy resting place, and duly repaired. In 1957 it was one of the Kings to be given a double chimney, but it was withdrawn at Cardiff Canton in November 1962, with 1,663,271 miles on the clock and later scrapped at Bird's yard in Newport. It is seen here towards the end of its working life at Old Oak Common.
Trans-Pennine Archive (W214)

Above: If the GWR had its Kings, it also had its pawns, in the form of the diminutive 2-6-2T for the Vale of Rheidol Railway. Seen outside its Aberystwyth shed, No.8 *Llywelyn* sits beneath a much smaller water tower than that seen in the previous view. Of the line's three steam engines, No.8 seems to have been the most camera shy, as most work usually fell to No.7 *Owain Glyndwr* or No.9 *Prince of Wales*. *Trans-Pennine Archive* (NG43)

Right: No visit to the Cambrian Coast, nor indeed any book on the GWR, could be complete without a picture of the superb bridge at Barmouth. The railway and pedestrian bridge was built in 1867 and the original structure had a drawbridge, where a section of the structure was winched back onto the northern side of the bridge. This was, of course, before a swing-bridge section was inserted in 1901. *Trans-Pennine Archive* (V12)

EVERY PICTURE tells a thousand words, or so they say, and thanks to the combined talents of photographers who have supplied material to both the Strathwood and Trans-Pennine archives, we have a lot to say in future volumes. Of course it would not have been possible to tell this story without the kind co-operation of the contributors named in the credits shown in this book. To those and all those who captured British Railways In Colour, we say a massive thank you! However mere words are never enough, and we hope that the ongoing series will provide a testimony to their far-sighted work. This view of an Autocar working on 14th September 1964 is typical of GWR branches around the network, at least at the first glance. Normally this particular duty fell to an 0-4-2T but here we see a non-auto-fitted Class 57xx 0-6-0PT, 9606, at Chalford. The engine spent only a few weeks at Gloucester Horton Road (85B) so its appearance on this turn is quite rare! *Chris Forrest* (W250)

In conclusion, can we offer a reminder that all of these published shots are available to purchase as superb duplicate slide copies direct from Strathwood. The code number at the end of each slide indicates its catalogue number, and also the name of the photographer whose work we felt warranted inclusion.

To get your copy of the extensive catalogue listing of these and many thousands of other shots available in fabulous colour, please send £5.00 to: -

> Strathwood Limited
> Kirkland House, Bruce Street, Whithorn.
> Dumfries & Galloway DG8 8PY

Or visit the websites: -

www.strathwood.com or www.railwayslide.co.uk.

In return we will send the collector's catalogue, complete with sample slide, post free to UK address (overseas add £2.50).